I0201246

RECITATIONS IN RHYME

Robert F. McMeekin

Recitations in Rhyme

Copyright © 2012 by Robert F. McMeekin

All rights reserved. No part of this book may be reproduced or transmitted in any form or by any means without written permission of the author.

ISBN 9781620501781

To all of the girls I ever loved.

Contents

Bent

She smiled and winked as she sallied on by
Was she smiling at me? I wonder why

She was gorgeous-she smiled at me
A breath of spring-she winked at me

I saw her again-I got a wink and a smile
I blushed and turned red-I was speechless for a while

Blonde and blue-eyed five feet two
If I see her again, I'll know what to do

I did see her again- I was tongue tied and shy
She gave me a note with her name and number-I let out a sigh

How could I tell her, what would I say
I'll just have to tell her- I'm engaged to Ray!

Robert F. McMeekin

The Autumn Of My Years

The Autumn of my years, the winter of our discontent, the spring of
my youth, who penned these words-they are far from the truth.

I've had a good life, though short it may be
I've a few years left-and that's the key

Would that I knew then what I know now
Life would have different-that I would vow

I would have planned for the future and not lived for today
It wasn't all bad though, living that way

Fun and games do not a nest egg make
But a little planning may save the day yet

A penny saved is a penny earned
Ah what the heck-my bridges are already burned

Why Dogs Bark At The Mailman

Every day I pick up the mail
Every day my little dog wags his tail

Bills and ads maybe a letter-but all for me
He watches and waits, gazing hopefully

He barks at the mailman, where's my letter?
He's never gotten any mail and it won't get better

Sad and unhappy, he jumps into his bed
No Mail today, maybe tomorrow, he thinks in his head

He nears the mailman a few doors away
He runs to the door and barks his way

No mail today-the mailman smiles
And that's why he barks at him-pure animal wiles

Robert F. McMeekin

Count My Blessings

Each morn I wake and count my blessings
I'm alive and well and that's worth professing

My plate is full-no worries to dread
My family beside me- a roof overhead

Life's been good to me, I give thanks every day
It's time to share my bounty-I really do care

To those in need I'm willing to share
A helping hand-I really do care

You need a hand-I'll give you mine
To those in need, you'll do just fine

Greed and vice are all around
Let's wipe them out and stomp them aground

Then next morn when we're all awake
We'll all give thanks for heaven's sake

L.A. Is My Beat

I write no tickets unless I'm told
I arrest no felons unless they're old

I write no reports unless Sarge is there
I see no crime-why should I care?

I use all my sick days-each and every year
I'll probably make Sgt.,so you can buy me a beer

I work graveyards so I can sleep in the hole
My partner handles my court cases-100% no show is my goal

I have a dozen commendations 'cause my partner is alert
Any pretty girls on my beat with them I must flirt

I shop in my uniform and expect a police discount
I only eat where they feed me-freebies are too many to count

I can't quit smoking 'cause the smokes are free
I'm a career police officer-I
Love this job as anyone can see

Robert F. McMeekin

The Girl For Me Only

A cup of coffee, a glass of wine
The girl for me only, tell her she's mine

A day at the beach, a walk in the park
The girl for me only, tell her she's mine

Dinner for two, a nite on the town
The girl for me only, tell her she's mine

A drive in the country, a kiss in the dark
The girl for me only, tell her she's mine

A walk down the aisle, I do-'til death do us part
The girl for me only, now I know she's mine

Ah, But That's Life

You'll meet a girl, You'll like that girl
You'll ask her for her hand, she'll show you her band
Ah-but that's life, ah-but that's life

You'll look again, like about ten
The one you'll love will be a turtle dove
Ah-but that's life, ah-but that's life

You'll settle down-look around
One day you'll see the girl that's to be
You'll marry her and raise a family
Ah-but that's life, ah-but that's life

The years fly by, you've grown old and grey
You'll take her hand, there are no regrets
Not even for a day
Ah-but that's life, ah-but it was a great life

Robert F. McMeekin

That's What Life's About

As I was walking down the street a pretty girl passed me by
I looked at her and then I saw her start to cry

I said to her, "It's a gorgeous day-why so sad?"
"My boyfriend left me- I feel so bad."

Dry your tears and come with me- I have your cure
You know me not-what makes you so sure?

I've been there myself-I know how you feel
We had a cup and some cherry pie-no big deal

We talked a bit and rambled on and then she smiled
The tension was gone as were the tears-she was no longer riled

I walked her home and asked her out
She said, "I'd like that, that's what life is all about."

It Started To Rain-
I Didn't Complain

I was out one day for a walk in the park
It was rainy and gloomy and the sky was dark

I spotted an owl as he gave me a hoot
The cricket band was off on a toot

Sitting on the bench was a girl outta sight
Her hair was a muss and her face a fright

There was thunder and lightning and it started to rain
My clothes were soaked but I didn't complain

I fell in love on a dark, rainy day
I sat next to her but had nothing to say

She smiled at me and said, "I like the rain.
I'm glad you stopped by- my name is Jane"

We sat for a while 'til the sun came out
I took her hand and held her close, we were in love without a doubt

Robert F. McMeekin

The Years Flow By

Time after time, day after day
The years flow by-I lived my way

School yesterday-a career gone by
Life's moved on, the memories never die

Old friends call or drop a line
Where did it go-this life of mine

Pretty girls I chased for love and fun
They came and went until I married one

Now my kids are my life
They live as I did and cause me strife

I've been there girl, live and learn
You're on your own, now it's your turn

I'm in the autumn of my years
My life's flown by-I shed no tears

Class Action

The prettiest girl I've ever seen sat next to me in class today. She smiled at me-her eyes were laughing, smiled again as I blushed away

She said "My pens gone dry, can I borrow yours, I'll give it right back." First she smiled at me-then she talked to me-I'm flying now and way off track.

I stared at her-my heart skipped a beat. She smiled again and winked at me-if this is love-I'm in heat

The class was over-I heard not a word
She said, "Here's your pen." But not a word I heard

She got up to leave and said, "Thank you Bob."
SHE KNEW MY NAME-I knew not hers-I ran after her –right through the mob

Keep my pen but tell me your name
She said, "My name is Sam but my parents are to blame."
Well, Sam sez I- "I like your name"
"I'll buy you coffee- I'm game if you're game."

We went for coffee and dinner and drinks we had
The story ended and happily I might add
A fine romance began that nite
We were pinned in a month and things were just rite

Robert F. McMeekin

This Land was Built
By You & Me

America, America, God shed his grace on thee
The highways, the bridges, the tunnels are all built by you and me

From the New York Islands to the Golden Gate
The cities, the hi-rises are all an American trait

The universities, the malls were all started from a blueprint
The guys that drew them, to the workers who read them put in their
stint

The fighters, the bombers, the mighty ships at sea
The tanks and jeeps, the six-bys were built to keep is free

Everything that man constructs were built by construction men
The homes we live in-the stores we shop in
Everything that makes living "in like Flynn"

This land around us was built by you and me
So-be proud to be a construction worker just like me and thee

CUBA

Men of honor, Boys in the hood
Show me the money, oh, that was good
In Radio he showed me his range
A nice guy, in Hollywood that is strange
In his chosen field, he's at the top of his game
He married his high school sweetheart, Sara's her name
They brought forth Spencer, Mason, and Piper
How proud he must ne, ever so hyper
I'm proud of him, proud to call him a friend
This is just the beginning
He's a long way from the end….

Happy birthday Cuba!!!!

Robert F. McMeekin

The Queen Of Halloween

It was late in October, the moon did shine
It was dark and eerie, about a quarter to nine
I heard a scream that sent chills down my spine
Another scream! And another! All was not fine

Then I saw it. It gave me a fright
It was a body hanging high in the night

I locked the door. I pulled down the shade
I turned up the lights…then watched them fade

My dog ran behind me, more scared than I,
We huddled together-both scared but, why?

More screams; then more. I peeked out the door
There was blood in the doorway; then the hanging body began to soar
I tripped over my dog and fell to the floor,
He ran behind me and barked at the door

The door flew open and let in the mist
I saw her then as I tightened my fist
It was a witch! The witch of Halloween
The she smiled. I remembered she-was my witch, she was my Queen!

14

God Bless America

See the foliage in New England in the fall
See Yosemite and the redwoods ever so tall

Walk down the halls of the White House and feel a sense of what
made this country so great
Walk down Bourbon Street and have some jambalaya by the plate

See the Atlantic and the Pacific and ole man Mississippi
See Niagra, Lake George, and the mighty Missouri
Drive through the Painted Desert and the Petrified Forest
See the great plains of the Midwest and watch a fall harvest

See the Grand Canyon and Yellowstone and our other majestic fields
of grain
Drive through the Mojave and great American deserts and the Snake
River on a train

See New York, Boston, Minneapolis/St. Paul and Atlanta
And when you're done you'll know why God did bless America

Robert F. McMeekin

Yesterday

I can't believe I'm seventy two
Just the other day I was dating you

Dinner and a show, a drink and a dance
The nites almost over- a little romance

Whatever happened to a nite out with the boys
Softball and bowling- drinking and noise

Sports cars and girls-it was great- I'll call you
Bar hopping and deal shopping, a waistline that grew

Marriage and kids- a home of my own
Two weeks in the country-now the kids have grown

Don't get around much anymore
I'm old and grey-with memories galore

Yesterday I Was Sixteen

I woke up today and what did I see
I saw myself at seventy three

How can that be-yesterday I was sixteen
I got my drivers license and drove all over just to be seen

I smoked cigarettes 'cause I was tough
My girl was small and pretty and always telling me "that's enough"

Then I was in college- a great place to be
Pretty girls and kegs of beer-college was made for me

Then I found out I was supposed to go to class
I got kicked out-kicked out on my ass

Three in the Corps, I shoulda gone to class
An honorable discharge- reup my ass

Twenty years and twenty minutes with the LAPD
I was a hot dog, than the man- NO! you listen to me

Oh yeah, I was married twice and had three girls
I shitcanned the wives but kept my pearls

I'm retired now and a pension I get
It still seems like yesterday but I can't complain yet

40!!!

I have a friend who's at the top of his game
He woke up today with a 40 before his name

Happy birthday sez she
40! Sez he

Yesterday I was 16 and cutting classes at North Hollywood
I can remember break dancing and Boyz in the Hood

I can recall my big payday- "show me the money!"
Oh yeah- I had two sons and married my high school honey

It was the electronic age and he had "Radio"
The thirties flew by- A daughter was born and he was big daddio

40! How can that be?
Is that gray hair that I do see?

Don't feel to bad- don't be mad
Go make a movie-life ain't so bad

Look Around Thee

I see blue skies all day
I see blue stars all nite

I see the sunrise in the morn
I see the sunset in the eve

I see the moonrise at dusk
I see the moonset at dawn

I see the snowcapped mountains
I see the trees in the forest

I see the waves breaking on the shore
I see the lakes and rivers-all within reach

I see skyscrapers and city lites
I see fields growing as far as I can see

I hear birds in the tree
I see all this and it's all free
You ask "how's it going?"- I reply "look around thee."

Tammi

I have a daughter, her name is Tammi
She has a good heart and God dami
She's ready to help with razzmatazz
What's hers is yours and all that jazz
She is a good soul and there for you
Good natured for all- never so few
A friend today, a friend for life
Through thick and thin, good times or strife
She's great with kids, a really good friend
You can count on Tammi, a really good trend

If

If I could fly, I'd fly on high
If I could climb a tree, I'd take you to the top with me

If I could swim the sea, I'd swim with you to Tahiti
We'd rest in Bermuda, then swim to Bali

If I were a rich man
I'd make you a rich woman

If I were a man who was smart
I'd take your hand and give you my heart

If I were brave & strong
I'd carry you off with me and you I'd save

If I could write a book
You'd be my queen and we'd live by a brook

If I could have my way
I'd be with you each and every day

If this story had an end
It would end with you as my wife and friend

God's Country

A little log cabin with a stream drifting by
Deep in the woods with trees whispering hi

A lake down the road and you nearby
What more could I want- a kiss and a sigh

The moon and the stars out every nite
The sun thru the trees, oh what a sight

I'm in God's country and I want you with me
Share the joys as plain as can be

Wake up each morn and start out the day
End up each nite with you I do pray

Take My Hand

I see sunshine and pretty flowers
I see pretty girls and sunshowers

Off in the distance, the end of the rainbow
My pot of gold way down low

Walk with me and brighten my day
Stay with me and light the way

Join with me and two are one
Be with me 'til life is done

You made my day- you made my nite
How can I thank you for fancy and flight

Take my hand as we cross into eternity
Together in life and again in infinity

Robert F. McMeekin

Twenty Years And Twenty Minutes

How proud I am, how proud I be
A retired vet of the LAPD

Seventy six guys were in our class
Sixty three graduated to crush crime enmasse

Five went to Hollywood and got lost in the hills
Somehow we survived the booze, broads and pills

Then onto Wilshire, the Miracle Mile
The jungle, the hookers on Adams- all bring back a smile

Next I tried AID and car crashes and DUI
Freeway flyers, accident stats and the reason why

Back to Hollywood, I was a police officer now
The felony car, vice and narc, I knew how

Promoted to sergeant- I was on my way
Don't do as I do- just do as I say

Captains adjutant- out of the field, a suit at last
Then I was in jail- twenty years gone by- it had been a blast

I'm retired now- with memories galore
I've never been sorry that I enforced the law

Still In Love

While at college I met a girl
We started to date- she was a pearl

We fell in love and planned to wed
We couldn't wait so we moved in together instead

Then I was drafted- to war I was sent
The war raged on- through hell I went

Three years it lasted-they said we won
Finally I got home-my romance was done

She'd married and moved away she did
Where she moved, no one knew-but she had a kid

I thought of her often, even wished her well
Someone took my place while I was in hell

Twenty years went by- then a knock at the door
She was standing there- lovely, at twenty four

"I'm your daughter." She said and smiled at me
No doubt about- I was still in love you see

Robert F. McMeekin

Friendly Valley

I was walking my dog along Avenue of The Oaks
When I saw some neighbors who seemed like kindly folks

They pet my dog whose name was Cholo
He wagged his tail-got no treat and continued solo

We walked by a beautiful golf course
Where he chased a coyote with energy and force

Next we saw a pool with ducks in for a swim
Then a lawn bowling green where we bowled on a whim

We came to a street named Whispering Leaves
My dog marked every tree and pole I do believes

Everywhere we walked there was grass and pretty flowers
The sun was shining-the birds sang with gusto and power

This was a village called Friendly Valley
The last stop before Eternal Valley

Just We Two

It was a dark and gloomy day
Not a ray of sunshine and rain was on the way

Then I heard thunder- and more thunder and saw lightning
A car came racing up and stopped before a crash

A very pretty girl jumped out and said, "Have you seen my dog Jane?
She got loose and I must find her before the rain."

"You take the high road and I'll take the low."
Off we went as the rain increased and the wind did blow

Two blocks away I spotted Jane-her leash was caught in a sewer drain
She was cold and shivering and her coat was soaked with rain

I undid the leash and picked up Jane and headed home
I saw the pretty girl and said, "May I borrow your comb?"

There were tears in her eyes but her face lit up with a happy smile
She hugged Jane whose tail was wagging all the while

She gave me a hug and said, "How can I thank you?"
That's easy sez I –dinner tonite- Just we two.

Robert F. McMeekin

The Sound Of Music

The music sang the words of my alltime favorite song
The drums and brass made it an old time sing along

The eighty eight keys made me close my eyes
The drums added a beat at the lows and highs

The sound said it all-from beginning to end
The rhythm set the tune and a message it did send

Nothing says it better than a nicely worded song
And the music sings the words and you'll never get 'em wrong

If school books were written by Irving Berlin and Lerner and Lowe
People everywhere would be singing their studies-say it isn't so

There are happy songs and sad songs, there are love songs and
songs of war
You can sing along or hum along and easily follow the score

So-if you can send a message and make them understand
Set the words to music and sing it out loud and everything will be grand

Never

The prettiest girl I'll never know
Just walked past and said hello

The sweetest lass I'll never see
Was in my dream waving at me

The nicest girl I've never met
Sang to me on the Internet

The only girl I'll never love
Broke my heart with no lark or no dove

The cutest wench I'll never date
Stood me up and was an hour late

The loveliest girl I didn't meet
Gave me the boot with both her feet

Then I woke from my nitemare
My love beside me- smiling with love and care

Robert F. McMeekin

Down By The Riverside

I saw a pretty little girl- down by the riverside
I walked right up to her-and asked her if she'd like a ride

She sized me up-and sized me down
Then she smiled and winked and said, "I'm headed to town."

I offered my arm and told her my name
She took my arm and said, "You're not to blame."

We drove to town and stopped at a bar
She said, "I'll go in and order drinks you go park the car."

We had some drinks and bar snacks too
Then we danced and pitched some woo

That's how it all started, it's never ended
The moral of this story's clear-don't do as I do-do as I did

You Can't Have It All

I see blue skies and birds on the fly
I see trees of green and birds flying high

I see flowers in bloom and fields of green
I hear the robins song and bees with their queen

What I don't see are trees without leaves and snow on the ground
What I miss are cold winter nites and snowflakes all around

I miss the thunder and lightning that flashes up high
Walking in the rain and raindrops in each eye

I love it in Malibu and dear old Cape Cod
I like the Grand Canyon and Martha's Vineyod

You can't have it all but you can try
You can vacation back east and then say bye-bye

You can stay alive in the northeast or even the southwest
You can stay in the old south but west is the best

Robert F. McMeekin

We Two

Moonlite and music- a pretty girl-and dancing
Such a pretty girl-no lites and romancing

A nite for love- a nite for romance
Breakfast in bed then a strut and a prance

A day at the beach, a stroll in the park
Dinner for two-dancing 'til dark

Back in the grind, a start of a new week
Monday thru Friday then starting to peak

A trip to the country, a cabin in the woods
Smell the fresh air, a lazy weekend with all the goods

Life is just great and it's all because of you
Promise me you'll stay with me forever-just we two

The Girl Down The Street

There was a pretty girl who lived down the street
My goal in life was for her I meet

I thought and thought and came up with a plan
I'd just walk up to her and say "Hi, my name is Dan."

I waited for my chance but it did not appear
One day went by-then two-how could she just disappear

On the third day, I finally saw her
As we approached I mumbled and she said, "Excuse me sir."

Now I was blushing but finally said, "Hi, my name is Dan."
She smiled and held out her hand saying, "I'm Mary Moran."

I shook her hand and couldn't let go
"Would you like to go to the opera, a museum, or listen to music
sweet and low?"

She laughed and said, "How about a show?"
To a show we went, I was no longer blushing-I was all aglow

After the show, we dated a while and then went steady
After a few months, I popped the question and she said, "Whenever
you're ready."

Robert F. McMeekin

Somewhere Along The Way

Every day there's some sunshine and a little bit of rain too
I've had some good days and bad days were a few

I'm on a good roll on this very day
I have a date with a very pretty girl and we're gonna see a play

Maybe we'll stop for dinner somewhere along the way
After the play, we'll stop for a drink somewhere along the way

Dinner was great but we had a flat tire on the way to the play
We never had a drink because we had a flat tire somewhere along
the way

Now I'm on a bad day roll as the day turned to nite
Me and my pretty girl are stuck out nowhere and that's our sorry plight

Now our nite is ruined and we're a long way from home
There were no cabs around and we've a long way to roam

Our feet were killing us and there was no place to stay
And so ends our story as we got stuck- somewhere along the way

Where Are The Years

Where have they gone? All of the years…..
Yesterday I was in school, I remember the cheers

Then I was in college, I remember it well
Away from home Sigma Chi I would yell

I joined the Marines, the few, the proud, the best
I did my tour, stayed out west

I was married once, I was married twice
I had three girls, they were worth the price

I was a cop, I wore blue
The years flew by, in stature I grew

Now I'm retired, a pension I get
My girls are grown, my obligations are met

I lived my life, I shed no tears
Where have they gone? Where are the years?

Robert F. McMeekin

Growing Old

Growing old, growing old
It's gonna be great, so I've been told

Well, I don't agree, it's not for me
I'd rather be twenty, that's where I wanna be

I wanna laugh and have fun and stay out all nite
I wanna chase the girls and be their delight

I wanna play ball and golf and bowl
I wanna go out with the boys and bare my soul

I wanna kiss and make up and all that jazz
I wanna hold you all night and razz a ma tazz

But I did that once! I remember now!
It seemed like fun but I can't remember why or how

Nostalgia's allright, it's really a trip
But I'd rather be with you and wait for our ship

I want our kids to grow up and start their quest
Be doctors or lawyers but do their darned best

If I had to do it over, I'd do it all again
I'd choose you again but I'd think back now and then

It's fun to remember and hard to forget
We did grow old together! I have no regret

Valentine's Day

It's Valentine's Day and I bought no gift
I'd better get cracking to avoid a rift

I drove downtown where the stores were open
Shopping's a chore and I only have ones and a ten

What should I buy-what will she like?
Candy is dandy or a puppy named Spike

I shopped for an hour and had no clue
Then I saw it- it was her just due

Now it was late as I raced back home
I already had a card with a very nice poem

I made it home and the lite was still on
I rushed in the house to find her gone

Then I heard a noise in the yard
I saw her wagging a tail and chewing her card

Robert F. McMeekin

At Any Rate

It's after eight
I'm waiting for my date

Nothing new, she's always late
One of these days I ain't gonna wait
She's very pretty- I can't give her the gate

If I did- it's me I would hate
So here I sit, sealing my fate
With nothing to do-the whole pie I ate

I fell asleep after cleaning the plate
In she comes with a cat in a crate

She smiled at me, saying, "I love you Nate."
That's okay- I love you Kate

We hugged and kissed as was our trait
She whispered in my ear, "I'll be your mate."
That was it- she took the bait
I'll marry her soon at any rate

A Long Time Ago

I remember when there were locomotives and planes with props
Before CSI and evidence technicians, our streets were patrolled by
cops

I was a one finger typist and the first to own a Bomar Brain
I was happy to dial a phone and content to travel by train

Gas was 15c a gallon and Wings 13c a pack
Coffee was a nickel and if you needed a copy, it took forever and left
ink on the back

College meant campus, coeds and fun
Four years of study and then you were done

Dancing was together-she'd sing in your ear
Christmas ended the season-then Happy New Year

You drove a Ford or Chevy or sometimes a Plymouth or Dodge
You took your girl to a movie and maybe a drink at the lodge

Life was simpler a long time ago
I remember it well-I miss it so

Does She Ever Think Of Me?

I thought about her again today
My first true love- who sent me away

I was crazy about her- but she loved my friend
Does she ever think of me-my heart she did bend

I thought of her often- many years after we parted
She was so pretty- I was never sorry we started

She broke my heart but I wish her well
Did she keep her looks and her figure so swell

I'd love to see her again but know not where to look
It's been over fifty years and different paths we took

I hope her life was as good as mine
I still think of her but my life is fine

My Wish

I wish I may I wish I might
Love the girl I met tonite

I saw her there with a tear in her eye
I felt so bad-it hurt to see her cry

I said, "Cry no more, it makes me sad
To see a pretty girl who feels so bad."

She brushed a tear from her eye
Then she smiled- I know not why

She said, "You're very nice, it's plain to see
I've lost my love- it was not meant to be."

"He loves another and lied to me
You seem nice but I'm poor company."

Here's my number, call me later
I could wait no more, I called to date her

And date her I did-again and again
She was only eight and I was ten

Robert F. McMeekin

A Little Slice Of Heaven

A little slice of heaven and the deed states it's mine
Sunshine in the fields and that makes it very, very fine

There's a brook bubbling on the boundary to the west
There's a snow capped mountain to the east just beyond the crest

There's no one nearby so we can do as we please
The wildlife amble by content and at ease

There's a pretty girl humming inside as she's making dinner
There's a dog barking playfully and the kids think he's a winner

Nitefall is upon us and the moon is glowing brightly
The stars begin to twinkle which makes the heavens very sightly

This is our bit of heaven, hers and mine
As we sit for a dinner we thank the Lord for our life with a toast from
the vine

This is where we wanna be-this is where we're gonna stay
Thank thee Lord- share our toast-listen as we pray

Colors Marie

My little dog died last nite
She tried so hard but lost the fite

She brought me joy for so many a year
She shared our home so she was always near

She loved the yard and the warm bright sun
She never strayed far but the squirrels she'd chase-oh what fun

She gave me her love and was so very loyal
She'd wait for me and when I got home you'd think I was royal

When she wanted attention-she'd paw the air
She loved when I pet her-she made me care

I miss her so- dear Colors Marie
I'm going in the yard and plant her a tree

Robert F. McMeekin

Ready For Hell

When I was young and in my prime
I was a handsome lad and had girls all the time

As I grew older, I still kept my looks and often had my way
There were still plenty of girls but I often missed a day

Now that I'm older and somewhat gray
I'm still a charmer and have more money for a roll in the hay

As the days grow shorter and I am still alone
I like it that way-in fact-I threw away my trusty cell phone

I have fondest memories of the days gone by
I often think of you & Bobbi & Sue & oh, yes a girl name Vy

Life has been good and I've aged quite well
I have no regrets, I enjoyed my life and I'm ready for hell

We Both Did Care

There were tears in her eyes
As we said our goodbyes

It was a summer romance and love at first sight
I got a hug and a kiss and a promise she'd write

No letter for weeks, for months, for years
I thought if her often, especially after a few beers

Then out of the blue-a letter came through
"I was married when we met but I was afraid to tell you"

"I'm a widow now but I always thought of you
I'll be in town next week but I'm just passing thru"

"I'd love to see you and meet for a drink"
And meet her I did and not just for a drink

The years had been kind to us both-the spark was still there
She felt the same way-we both did really care

Robert F. McMeekin

Life's Been Good

I never cared about being a celebrity
I was really happy just being me

I never wanted a mansion high in the hills
I was just pleased with a cottage for two and no overdue bills

Gold and diamonds were never my thing
I only needed a watch that kept good time and my college class ring

A Rolls Royce was never my dream
But a little sports car the color of cream

Gorgeous movie queens were nice on the screen
The little girl I married would always be my queen

Life's been good and somewhere along the way
You gave me all of those things and everything was okay

I thank thee dear for a lifetime so rare
The twilights on us and that's okay- 'cause I know you did care

Home

See the trees along the way
Hear the birds-listen to what they say

See the pretty flowers in the gardens all around
Watch the butterflies flitting without a sound

A gentle breeze moves the air
Crickets chirp 'cause they don't care

I seldom hear a car horn blare
No graffiti on the walls anywhere

Take your dog for a walk
Laugh as the squirrels run up a tree and gawk

Walk on home-greeting neighbors as you pass by
It's great living here-it's ice cream and apple pie

Robert F. McMeekin

It's Been A Good Life

I do no work-I do what I like
I stare at the girls- especially one named Mike

I drive a fancy car, own my own home
I go where I please and casually roam

I'm a dirty old man with no worries or stress
I have enough money and more, I must confess

Allows me to play and pay for my mess
I make no apologies each day as I undress

I am what I am and sleep like a baby
I dream pleasant dreams, maybe just maybe

I'll wake up each morning, start another day
I feel good about myself 'cause I did it my way

If I had it to do over, I'd do it the same
If I did all wrong, I'd only have me to blame

Hale And Hearty

I sip no scotch- I drink no beers
I walk everywhere-ride a bike with gears

I watch my diet-if the food tastes good-I do not eat
Sugar is a no-no, cheesecake my annual treat

Picnics are fun but not for me
Celery and carrots are great snacks you see

I stay out of the sun, don't go in the rain
I'm up at daylite-when it's dark-I train

I take short trips by car, long trips by plane
I bring my own snacks-now ain't that a pain

I'm healthy and shipshape-the envy of my peers
I've outlived all my friends, I'm alive beyond my years

I followed all of the rules and hated every bit
Am I having any fun-don't believe that shit!

Robert F. McMeekin

Her Look, Her Smile

She had a look about her then
Her wink would always tell me when
She'd take my hand and lead the way
I knew right then just what to say
Soft and pretty with a vexing smile
I'd smile right back and linger awhile
The years flew by, we grew apart
She lost the smile she had from the start
Then she was gone, in heaven I know
I can see her smile, I loved her so

I'll Drink To That

In a few days I'll be 77 and here's what I think
I never tire of the Star Spangled Banner- even after a drink

God Bless America brings a tear to my eye
I've been to all fifty states-it's so long-never goodbye

The world loves the Hanging Gardens and the magnificent Sphinx
I'll take the Grand Canyon and holding hands with a minx

A walk in the garden-a day in the park
The sand under our feet- a kiss in the dark

A weekend in the country-the moon and stars
Walking on a cloud on Jupiter and Mars

You by my side- a family to raise
America the beautiful- I'll sing her praise

Growing old together- the golden years
It's been a great ride-I'll drink to that with a few beers

Fred

It was a grand and a glorious day
Little Bobby and Freddie were born
Laughing all the way

It was the 6th of November,1934
Stocks were soaring and headed for more

Our nation was at peace-Brooklyn was the place
The recession was behind us- Bob and Fred were in the chase

They grew up in Brooklyn then headed west
They settled in L.A.- ready to begin their quest

Fred sold car insurance and Bob enforced the law
Bob retired from the LAPD and Fred enforced the law

They both retired and pensions they got
The life of Riley and all that rot

Then Fred got cancer and left too soon
He's paving the way for Bob while resting on the moon.

9/10/11

I watched you grow over many, many years
You had the most colorful hair of all your peers

I was happy and proud when a hairdresser you became
I had visions of scissors and combs bringing you fame

I was pleasantly surprised when a boyfriend you had
When you said you were to be married, I was certainly glad

Then you set a date so far away of 9/10/11
I saw it as an omen and a little bit of heaven

Your day is now here and you shall be man and wife
Keep this pearl for the rest of your life

Love your man and raise a family
Be together as one and your life will be free

There is nothing more important than those you love
Be happy and loving and your life will be a lark and a dove

Robert F. McMeekin

The Bachelor

I cannot figure what is the matter with me
I cannot get her out of my mind, it's a mystery

I saw her today and as I approached, she smiled at me
She smiled at me, I cannot get her out of my memory

She was very pretty- I think I'm in love
I must see her again, my heart is floating just like a dove

I walked that same street for at least a week
I did not see her again, not even a peek

Then one nite I saw her walking her collie
Meet her I must- meet her I shall-by golly

I followed her a while and crossed her path
I petted her dog-she smiled at me- you do the math

We dated awhile 'til her dog gave birth
I ran for my life-it was fun while it lasted-merry and mirth

Our Country

This is our country-yours and mine
The oceans, the prairies, the mountains so fine

I live by a lake, surrounded by a park
It's not in the city-so it must be country-on a lark

I'm free to be- I am what I want
I go where I please, my choice my haunt

I own my own house, it's free and clear
It's where I choose to live-content-without fear

It's all very legal-it's written in law
A legacy passed down- a guarantee without flaw

No terrorist can say this-they envy our life
They try to destroy your land and mine
Our message is clear-stay in your cave
Or you'll only know strife

Robert F. McMeekin

There She Goes

There she goes, down the street-the prettiest girl I've seen all week
I followed behind her down the street- a little game of hide and seek

She dropped her keys-they fell in the mud
I just happened by and grabbed her keys from the crud

I am her hero and claimed my due
A Broadway show and dinner for two

The show was fine-dinner was great
I took her home-it was really late

She kissed my cheek and said goodnite
The nite was fun then she was outta site

But I had her number firmly in hand
I'll call her tomorrow-she is my brand

Saving Irene

A pretty girl called me today
How do I know she was pretty-she stopped by when out my way

She was preaching religion-on me a waste of time
She gave me a Watchtower-surely not a crime

She pointed out an article on "Living Forever"
I said, "come in" and I undid the door lever

She said, "I can't stay-I've many souls to save"
"The only one that's important is right here" but he won't behave

"There's a place in hell for dirty old men" says she
"You got that right" says me

She turned on her heel-wasn't me she did save
She not only was pretty-she was fast and brave

Robert F. McMeekin

A Great Ride

Lay down beside me- help me thru the nite
When we wake, thank the Lord we made it from dark to lite

For fifty years you've been by my side
I thank you dear-it's been a great ride

When we were young, a handsome, happy pair were we
The world was ours-we took charge of what we wanted to be

Our kids grew up to make us proud
They're on their own now, moving up on a silver cloud

No time for us now, we're left alone now, it's really sad
Then again, it's no different now then it was for our mom and dad

So-we count our blessings and give our thanks
Life's been pretty good to us-it's time to close the ranks

Remember

The days seem shorter-the years are flying by
My life is nearly over and I really gave it a try

I remember yesterday like it was today
I wouldn't change a thing-thank heaven I wasn't gay

I'll never forget my first love-my love so true
I won't forget my second love or even my third and certainly not the
last few

I remember them well-I loved them all
It all went by so fast, mostly it was a ball

If I had it to do over I'd only change one thing
I never cared about being famous-hell, I couldn't even sing

I just hope you'll all remember me
'Cause I'll remember you and you and thee

Robert F. McMeekin

How Lucky Can I Be?

The girl of my dreams just walked on by
What'll I do-I've got to meet her, at least I must try

I followed her down the street for a block or two
She went into the house at the corner-222

I checked the mailbox, how clever of me
A name was on the side-that name was Lee

I ran all the way home and checked the phone book
I looked under Lee and there she was- same address- her name was
Brooke

I checked my computer every which way I could
I got lucky under Public Records-so far so good

She was 22 and single how lucky can I be
I had her address and phone number-the rest was up to me

I called her that nite and asked for a date
She said, "What took you so long?"-dinner would be great

From Playboy To Playdough

When I was young and really bold
I was a handsome lad- so I've been told

The girls all loved me which made me vain
I played the field and wouldn't commit which caused them pain

Some say cocky-I say confident
Some say playboy others say impudent

I drank with the boys and toasted the gals
A con man at heart-I had few pals

Then it happened as it always does
A very pretty lady set my heart abuzz

I was smitten-I was floating on air
She was so pretty-life is not fair

She changed my ways- for once I cared
Hen-pecked and on a leash- at last I was snared

Let There Be

Let there be the sun and the moon and a million bright stars
Let there be singing and dancing and a thousand guitars

Let there be pretty flowers and tall stately trees
Let there be fields and streams and a warm ocean breeze

Let there be peace in the valley and love all around
Let there be birds to sing and crops in the ground

Let there be good friends and neighbors and laughter abound
Let there be children playing and singing the only sound

Let there be fun and games and pretty girls to see
Let there be sunny days and quiet nites for you and me

Let there be bright days- plenty for all in a land that's free
Let there be freedom aplenty for me and thee

Don't let them take this from us-our way of life
Stand and be counted-every husband and wife

Dinner For Two

I was driving my Cad on the hiway of love
When a bolt of lightning struck me from above

I pulled to the side to see what was wrong
Just as a pretty lady aside me did pull along

"I've lost my way and I'm out of gas"
"Can you help me sir?" said this pretty little lass

"Lock up your car and get in my Cad"
"We'll get you some gas" said the tall handsome lad

It was love at first sight and he was glad of her plight
They drove for a ways and the day turned to nite

They found a gas station and filled up a 5 gallon can
They returned to her car and she said, "Thank you-my name is Ann"

"You're welcome I'm sure and here's your bill"
"Dinner for two and drinks to our fill"

"I have no money as I've run away you see"
"Follow me to that roadhouse so I can collect my fee"

"Dinner and drinks will be my treat"
"You're in my debt and I'm gonna collect- or my name ain't Clete"

Robert F. McMeekin

Ode To A Friend

In all the years I've been around and there have been many
My best friends have all been dogs bar any

They never argue, bitch, or nag
They're happy to be with me and when I pet them their tails do wag

If I get angry or mildly upset
They take the blame-on this you can bet

They never complain nor do they pout
They just want to please and jump for joy when we get ready to go out

If I give them a treat they're happy as can be
A little food and water is all they want-oh yeah and to be with me

There is no greater love than between man and his pets
It is said that after a few years we look alike and that's as good as it gets

I've had good buddies and many a girl friend
But me and my dog are together to the end

I Guess So

I just moved to the city and knew not a soul
To meet a pretty girl was now my new goal

So this is the plan-I'd get a dog and take him for a walk
I'll look for a pretty girl walking her dog and stop to talk

I'll be passive and let the dogs do all of the work
It worked like a charm-except my dog had a quirk

He'd chase after every dog-not all were led by a pretty girl
Then one morning I saw her- she was pretty as a pearl

My dog did his job-she smiled and was the first to talk
I blushed and was tongue tied but managed to say,
"See you tomorrow when we go for a walk"

The next morning finally came and there they were
Both dogs tails were wagging-she smiled and said, "good morning sir"

I was calm- I was cool, I returned her smile and said, "How about
some expresso?"
She smiled again and blinked a wink and said, "I guess so."

One year later my dog had pups-she was pregnant and ready to give life
We had been married for almost a year-she was still smiling and was
also my wife

Robert F. McMeekin

Take Me Out To The Ball Game

I took my girl to a Dodger game
The nite was warm and the fans were aflame

The Dodgers played well and were ahead by a run
My girl asked often "Is the game nearly over-this is no fun"

There was a meeting on the mound and all the infield was there
"Why don't they hurry-they don't seem to care"

"Can I have a ham sandwich, I don't want a Dodgers dog"
"Do they have any white wine, beer makes me agog"

"I don't want to stand up and sing"
"I don't care if it's the seventh inning fling."

"Why does that old guy keep going out to the pitcher?"
"Does he get paid extra and it makes him richer."

"The game must be over, everyone is moving down"
"Did the Dodgers win-who scored the winning touchdown?"

The moral of the story is easy-I don't go to High Tea
She's never been back to a game as you can readily see

You Are My Lady

I had a dream last night
When I woke to my delight
My dream came true
My dream was you

I wrote a song today
Read the words, see what I say
I love you dear, I want you near
Be my love, that's what you'll hear

I wrote you a letter and sent it by mail
When you read it, my words won't fail
They're written in ink and sealed with a sigh
You are my lady, I am your guy

Robert F. McMeekin

Stout Hearted Man

Give me some men, some stout hearted men
Who will fight for the right to marry other men

Gay rights and gay pride are all our inalienable rights
Where the boys are-out of the closet-men in tights

Two guys in love 'til death do us part
Growing old together-They've given each other their heart

The girls always stare when they pass on by
Their hearts are broken-these guys are gay-it makes them cry

Arm in arm-hand in hand-it makes me sick- especially when they
kiss
Two guys in love-now and forever-Mr. and Miss

Now it's legal in many of our states
It's now written in law-it's opened all the gates

There Was A Little Girl

There was a little girl who liked a little boy
There was a little boy who'd rather play with his favorite toy

She grew up-tall and fair
He didn't grow up and didn't care

Then one fine day a pretty little girl happened by
She saw the little boy who has also grown- it brought a tear to her eye

She stopped for a while and said, "Hi Tommy, how have you been?"
Tom looked up and then he smiled-it was his old friend Gwen

He threw away his toys and ran to her side
Then she realized- without his toys-he'd nowhere to hide

They walked down the street, hand in hand
Tommy grew up that day as they walked the land

The moral of this story is as plain as can be
Little boys finally grow up as one can plainly see

Robert F. McMeekin

She Felt Like A Cloud

I was writing a poem to read to the class
When a ghost came in with a shapely bad ass

I dropped my pen, jumped from the chair and fell on my rear
She winked at me as she floated by and said, "Have no fear."

Afraid I was not as she was quite a vision
Body by Fisher and nary a stitch on

She took my hand, kissed my cheek and I got a bust in the mouth
She whispered in my ear and then I knew she was from the south

She led me to bed and we lay down side by side
I closed my eyes and went along for the ride

She kissed both cheeks and then my lips
I had lust in my thoughts and my heart did flips

I reached for her side and caressed her head
She felt like a cloud as the alarm went off and I was alone in bed

Kelly The Patch

She cannot see, so she wears a patch
It makes no sense and doesn't match

I know why -there's a hole in her braino
I fixed it once with a can of draino

She is my niece, one of four
The 5 little k's, I watched them soar

Four girls and a boy, they weren't so bad
They stuck together, they were so rad

They still stick together, minus one
Kaylyn's in heaven watching the fun

This poem is for them but dedicated to Kelly
May the years be kind, like on the telly

Robert F. McMeekin

Walking My Dog

Me and my dog were taking a walk when he saw a pretty collie
We sauntered up closer and that pretty collie was led by a pretty dollie

My handsome mutt ain't got no class
He trotted right over and sniffed her ass

She smiled and said, "your dog is cute"
So yours said I, "and you to boot"

She blushed and blinked her eyes
But I knew she was pleased as we said our goodbyes

Thinking fast I said, "will you be this way tomorrow?"
She winked and said, "maybe I'll see you both on the 'morrow"

The nite dragged on, it was a very long wait
Finally it was time-I grabbed his leash-me and my dog both had a date

Mother Nature

It was a dark and gloomy day
There was thunder and lightning-the rain wasn't far away

Suddenly the skies lit up and the thunder roared
The lightning flashed and the rain poured

I locked the door and closed the blinds
I settled in for a long, dreary nite as heaven unwinds

The power went off and the furnace shut down
I sat in the dark and feared all outside would drown

Nite turned to day and it continued to rain
The outdoors were flooded and the fields could no longer drain

I dozed for a while and awoke under a ray of sun
I looked outside-the birds were singing and the squirrels were on the run

It was a beautiful day and a rainbow I did see
Mother Nature was no longer angry as she smiled down at me

Robert F. McMeekin

Election Day

It's Election Day-do we have a quorum?
Let me think-do I vote against or forum

Who's on the slate-who's good-who's an ass
What are the issues-I like her-He's so crass

Will they raise our fees and increase the dues
Who'll fix the leaks, who'll sing the blues

"I've got ants in the kitchen, my sink is overflowing
The paint is peeling, I want flowers that are always growing"

My smoke alarm is blasting-call the director, it's 2 am
I tripped on the sprinkler-a lawyer I am

I'll vote for him-I'm too busy to run
Let someone else do it –the Boards are no fun

Meet the candidates-listen to what they say-then vote
They do a great job and work for free and that you can quote

North of Forever

There was a pretty girl east of somewhere
There was a pretty girl west of nowhere

There were twin sisters north of forever
There was me south of everywhere

Which way should I go-which way do I dare
I chose east and had a great fling
Then I went west and did my thing

North was next on my compass
The end of the rainbow with a really bad ass

I climbed to a star and rested on a cloud
Then soft voices calling-their impact ever so loud

I was tired and worn with a tear in my eye
I headed for hell where I married my guy

Robert F. McMeekin

Friends

I was crazy about my best friend's gorgeous wife
She was a keeper and caused me nothing but strife

I stayed the course because friends are rare
No matter how I cut it, I really did care

The years went by-I kept my distance
He had a stroke-I was happy and sad in this one instance

I visited him often but he knew me no more
On one visit she kissed me and I finally did score

I felt bad for my friend but she stayed 'til the end
One day he passed but a message did send

"Take care of my wife-promise me my friend"
With a tear in my eye I whispered "on me you can depend"

And care for her I did-we were married that June
For many years after we sang a happy tune

www.ingramcontent.com/pod-product-compliance
Lightning Source LLC
Chambersburg PA
CBHW021211020426
42331CB00003B/312

* 9 7 8 1 6 2 0 5 0 9 1 0 4 *